LAF! Language Literature Lessons

Baroness d'Orczy

The Scarlet Pimpernel

by
Cheryl Couteaud

Copyright ©2014 Cheryl Couteaud
Tournesol Books a Division of Sweetwater Publications
PO Box 46 Culleoka, TN 38451 USA

No Part of this Publication may be reprinted, copied, etc., at any time.
For more copies please go to www.amazon.com to order

Baroness d'Orczy has manged to give us an intriguing spy novel of the late 1700's. Love, suspense, betrayal, heroism, deceit, and even humor all find their way into The Scarlet Pimpernel.

The baroness gives us a sense of what the aristocrats might have felt and lived like during the French Revolution. A fantastic tale of a hero, a girl, and a mission, however, our hero is a little less than what we think of when it comes to a spy and savior. None-the-less, he captures our hearts.

The Scarlet Pimpernel is the hero of the French "aristos" during the Revolution, but no one knows who he is- not even his own wife. A page turner, but is the tale accurate in depicting England, and France and such a harrowing time in history? I invite the reader to decide that for him or herself as you lose yourself in the adventure that is the League of the Scarlet Pimpernel.

This curriculum is sold individually to use with a combination of other novels, which you choose to fit your needs. This is meant to be used as a high school curriculum. For a compilation of novels to be used as a complete yearly lesson, please see the compiled book lists.

Curricula are offered for many great works of literature and for all grades. Language Arts is Fun! This curriculum gives your English student questions, creative writing assignments, essay topics, vocabulary lessons, and much, much, more. Literary terms, grammar rules, and essay outlines are found in the back of the book.

Thanks for purchasing! This curriculum can be used individually or in a co-op or tutorial setting. Reading great works of literature is required for English credit in all years of high school English and I feel you will find it meets all of your Language Arts needs. Enjoy! And have fun!

Contents

Short Answer Questions

Chaper I
Chapter II
ChapterIII
Chapter IV
Chapter V
Chapter VI
Chapter VII
Chapter VIII
Chapter IX
Chapter X
Chaper XI
Chapter XII
Chapter XIII
Chapter XIV
Chapter XV
Chapter XVI
Chapter XVII
Chapter XVIII
Chapter XIX
Chapter XX
Chaper XXI
Chapter XXII
Chapter XXIII
Chapter XXIV
Chapter XXV
Chapter XXVI
Chapter XXVII
Chapter XXVIII
Chapter XXIX
Chapter XXX
Chapter XXXI

Discussion Questions

Essay Topics

Research Topics

Vocabulary Assignment

Literary Challenge

Grammar Challenge

Appendix

Literary Terms
Essay Outline and Grading Guideline
Grammar Rules

Chapter I
Paris: September, 1792

1. Where and in what year does the story begin? (What is the setting?)

2. Are the first two sentences of the book even correct sentences? Why or why not? Why has the author chosen to begin her story this way?

Vocabulary:

aristocrat:_____
_____

"blue blood":_____
_____
_____

guillotine:_____
_____
_____

3. The first sentence emphasizes what? Who are these savages and what are they doing do you think?

4. Who is the "proud tyrant" she refers to that has since then raised his "undying monument to the nation's glory and his own vanity?"

5. We know the book takes place during the French Revolution- what is happening in the Revolution?

6. What literary device does the author use when she says, "Just a decade later the tyrant raises the monument...." and explain your answer.

7. How does the author feel about what the Revolution is doing to the "aristos," the aristocrats, the blue-bloods, and how do we know this?

8. How does Baroness d'Orczy defend the aristocrats? What does she say they have done for France?

9. What does she say about who is being guillotined that raises our sympathies?

10. What is the name of the group of people who are self appointed to catch the aristocrats and why is this ironic?

Vocabulary:
ci-devant: (fr) _____
satiety: _____
Citoyen: (fr) _____
pluck: _____
audacity: _____

11. Who is Bibot and what is he like?

12. Do the people like him? Why or why not?

13. Is he just? Is any of it just? Defend your answer.

14. How many people are guillotined each day?

15. Who makes up the citizen soldiers?

16. Who presides over the the committee of public safety and what does Orczy say of him?

17. What the names of the other two men over Bibot?

18. Describe the setting in your own words of the opening scene in detail or draw and label it here.

19. It's not just the aristos who get sent to the guillotine, but who else?

20. Why is the contraption nick named Madame Guillotine?

21. What is the bit stir in the city about?

22. Who is the man responsible for rescuing the aristos doomed to die, how is it done, and what is the "calling card" that he gives to Citoyen Foucquier-Tinville?

23. What is a Scarlet Pimpernel... (Don't look at the cover- those are poppies...)

24. Why do crowds come each evening to the West Gate to watch Bibot?

Vocabulary:

impudent: _____

_____

elusive: _____

_____

25. What is the story Bibot tells about how the family of aristos escapes?

26. What has the revolution managed to abolish in France but what still lives in the hearts of the people and who do they think the Scarlet Pimpernel is?

27. What does, "En avant" the carts mean?

28. Who does Bibot mostly talk to when it comes to the cart drivers?

29. Describe the woman Bibo talks to most as the carts leave the city. Where has he seen her before? What does she have with her? Who is sick in the back of the cart and with what ailment?

30. Describe the people watching the execution and what type of event does it seem to be. Do the people ever seem to work?

Draw the Scarlet Pimpernel disguised as the old woman here...

31. What does "Morbleu" mean?

32. What is the one thing that still is able to arouse fear in the hearts of the people?

33. How has the mood of the crowd changed since the cart has left?

34. Who does the cart driver turn out to be and what was his cargo?

35. What kind of man does Bibo seem to be?

36. What kind of man is the Scarlet Pimpernel?

Chapter II
Dover: "Fisherman's Rest"

1. Where is Dover?

2. What is the opening scene of the chapter?

Sally

3. What is Sally like? Describe her in great detail or draw a picture of her and label it. How many tankards can she carry at one time?

4. What is ironic about the name of the room where the quests are being served?

Mr. Jellyband

5. Describe in great detail the Fisherman's Rest and what does the author say about the place, the innkeeper, business, the employees, etc.

6. Describe Mr. Jellyband in great detail or draw and label him.

7. What does the author say about England, the continent (which would be continental Europe), and the rest of the world as a whole?

8. What are the recurring colors author continues to use?

9. What is the overall mood of the room? How is it such a contrast to the mood in the first chapter and are these people- the innkeeper and his family, the fishermen, etc. of the same or a different class than that of the citizens- "citoyens"- in France? How are they different?

10. The conversation of the guests is pleasant and what else... _____, showing they are not just average folk, but what is their trade, mostly, and is the author being ironic, or just funny?

11. How do the speech patterns, or diction, also give a clue to their class?

12. The late apples, pears, and plums are personified in passing, to emphasize the wetness of the weather, how?

13. Describe the conversation that follows between Mr. Hempseed and Mr. Jellyband.

14. How are the names of these men descriptive of who they are as well?

15. What is wrong with Mr. Hempseed's logic when it comes to the weather and government, even fruit and scripture? Is he an intelligent man, really?

16. How does Hempseed feel about what is happening in France and do his feelings reflect the feelings of the entire middle class and how is it different than those of the French middle class?

17. What does Hempseed refer to again when judging the rain in September? (Why is this ironic?)

Vocabulary:

peremptory: _____

_____

sarcastic: _____

_____

18. What do you think happens to Sally to make her jump and how or why does this get her father's attention?

19. What does he require her to do and what are his future plans for her?

20. Who is Jellyband expecting for dinner?

21. How does silly Hempseed feel about this, quoting what to make his point?

22. Jellyband this opportunity to get on his "favorite hobby horse." What is his position on the French Revolution and how does he make Hempseed feel?

23. What does he call the French?

24. Which customers become interested in Jellyband's speech and who are they?

25. What does the one gentleman say?

26. And how does Jellyband react?

27. What scripture does Hempseed quote?

28. Mr. Jellyband obviously reverences the king and he says he would be able to spot a frog-eater how?

29. What does the stranger do next? What good thing still comes from France? And note, this man is the only person in the "coffee room" drinking it.

30. The stranger assents to the fact that it is a "preposterous suggestion that anyone could ever upset Mr. Jellyband's firmly rooted opinions anent the utter worthlessness of the the inhabitants of the whole continent of Europe." Is this, in your opinion, foreshadowing, ironic foreshadowing, or merely a simple truth?

Vocabulary:

anent: _____

_____

preposterous: _____

_____

Chapter III
The Refugees

1. What is the general feeling in England of France's revolution- murder, as they call it?

2. Who is being murdered and what does the author mean when she says, "their only sin being their aristocratic name?" Why, do you think, is this a touchy subject for her?

3. What is England doing about it?

4. Who comes to the inn next and who si it that spots him first and announces him and how does he treat her?

Lord Antony

5. Describe in great detail or draw Lord Antony based on the description in the book.

6. How does he react to the domino playing gentlemen?

7. What does Lord Antony ask Hempseed and who does Hempseed blame for the answer?

8. What does Lord Antony announce and in whose reaction is he invested?

Vocabulary:

rueful: _____

_____

rubicund: _____

_____

9. What does Jellyband say of the stranger and how does Jellyband account for the man's rueful countenance?

10. Who else is coming to the inn?

11. What do we learn about Sir Percy and his lady from the brief conversation that ensues?

12. What do the men who are playing dominoes do when the carriage arrives?

13. Who is the lady who comes to the inn, whom Antony eagerly awaits? Describe her in great detail or draw and label her.

   The Comtesse

14. Who is the other young lady and who are the two men with them?

15. What feeling do you get from them- the women and alternately the men?

16. What mood does Harry Waite get into and why?

17. Describe the second man, who is the reason for Harry's jealousy.

18. Where do you suppose the husband and father of this recently escaped, French aristocratic family is?

Chapter IV
The League of the Scarlet Pimpernel

1. What do the two strangers do when they appear to have finished their game of dominoes?

2. Are the company really alone at last?

3. Who do they toast and why?

4. Where do we find out is the count, the husband and father to the rescued family?

5. What plans are in store for the count?

6. Do you think the countess made the right decision in coming to England with her children and leaving her husband behind in France? Why?

7. What does Orczy say of an Englishman's emotion?

8. Why is Suzanna shocked to heat there is a leader to the group of rescuers?

9. Who is the leader and why can't she meet him?

10. Describe a scarlet pimpernel and what is the meaning or significance of the hero naming himself after this flower?

11. Why do these men risk their lives to save the French aristocrats, according to Lord Antony?

    Vocabulary:

    dessinated: (this is a franglais word- the root being dessin) _____

    plebeian: _____

12. Does Madame la Comtesse believe him?

13. What would happen to the English men if they were caught in France rescuing aristos?

14. Why do the Comtesse and her children get saved?

15. What does she remember of the rescue?

16. What does she notice of the differences of the two countries, England and France?

17. How many members are in the league?

18. What does the Comtesse say about Marguerite St. Just?

19. Who is Marguerite St. Just and why is her name meaningful?

20. How does Suzanna know her?

21. What is known of Sir Percy and Lady Blakeney?

22. Does the Comtesse desire to meet Marguerite and why or why not?

23. Orczy uses words like "yokel" and phrases like "wet blanket" in her writing. Why have these words and phrases lasted?

24. What does this quote from the book mean and what type of literary device is it… "the comtesse encased in her plate armour of her aristocratic prejudices…"

25. How does the Comtesse portray herself now?

26. Why are Lord Antony and Jellyband uncomfortable?

27. How do the Blakeneys arrive at the inn?

Chapter V
Marguerite

1. What does Lord Antony jump up and try to do upon hearing the arrival of the Blakeneys?

2. How does the Comtesse react knowing the baroness is coming?

3. How does Suzanne feel about Lady Blakeney?

Vocabulary: (two french words)
sang-froid: _____
_____
soupçon: _____
_____

4. What does Jellyband do trying to avoid her unpleasant encounter?

5. Who is telling the story? The teller says, "mine host" throughout as if he/she is present, watching the story unfold, pay attention throughout the novel to see if it continues.

6. Describe in detail Marguerite Blakeney or draw and label her. (What is a marguerite in French?

Marguerite St. Juste- Baronesse, Lady Blakeney

7. How does Lady Blakeney react to and address the people present in the room?

8. What do Sir Anthony and Jellyband think as they watch the scene unfold of the two women's encounter?

9. Why does the Comtesse hate Lady Blakeney?

10. What does the Comtesse say to her daughter that makes everyone astonished?

Vocabulary:

scion: _____

insolence: _____

11. How does Marguerite respond to the Comtesse's rudeness?

fichu: _____

effusively: _____

12. How does lady Blakeney's demeanor change as she watches the Comtesse retreat down the passage?

13. Who notices? And what does she do?

14. What kind of look does Sir Antony follow Suzanne with and then what kind of look does he give to the Baroness?

15. What does the Baroness do?

16. Why was her laugh "forced and hard?"

17. Who steps forward to take up for her?

23

Chapter VI
An Exquisite of '92

1. Describe Lord Blakeney in great detail or draw and label him.

Lord Blakeney

2. What are the things Marguerite was known for in Paris?

3. Describe Lord and Lady Blakeney's marriage.

4. What do Marguerite's friends think of Blakeney and why do they think she married him?

5. Describe Sir Blakeney's personality and tell about where he was educated and why.

Vocabulary:

inane: _____

inanities: _____

imperturbable: _____

Bonhomme: _____

equanimity: _____

6. What does Orczy continue to say that Sir Percy and Lady Blakeney are the "leaders of English society?"

7. What does everyone think of Sir Blakeney's intelligence and that of his wife?

8. How do people feel Marguerite acts towards Sir Blakeney?

9. What is it that spoils Sir Percy's good looks?

10. Who tells Percy that his wife has been insulted?

11. Who answers Percy, which Percy proceeds to think is a crazed man and why?

12. What is the metaphor used to describe Percy and the Vicomte as the Vicomte is asking to settle the dispute with what?

13. How does Sir Percy deflect the challenge?

14. How does the Vicomte really speak English?

15. What is the joke Percy plays here- about the sword?

16. What is Percy's stance on duels?

17. What is the law's stance on duals?

Vocabulary:
bantam: _____
_____
choleric: _____
_____

18. How many saints are on the French? What does Lady Blakeney mean by this?

19. What does Percy say to folks about the type of people they are smuggling out of France?

20. What has Percy smuggled out of England?

21. Is this ironic foreshadowing? Why or why not?

22. For what is Percy so proud of himself?

23. What does Lady Blakeney do?

24. Sir Andrew has noticed someone in a new way- who?

Chapter VII
The Secret Orchard

1. What does Marguerite do once she's outside?

2. How does the weather reflect her mood?

3. What is Orczy's apparent opinion of the Revolution?

4. Who are the two men who approach the inn? Describe them in great detail or draw and label them.

Two men

5. How does Marguerite feel about the rebellion?

6. Where is Armand going?

7. Why does Marguerite warn him to be careful?

8. What does Marguerite give away about Percy's feelings towards her and why does he feel this way?

9. Armand gives a hint as to what?

10. Why does Percy not love Marguerite as much since he found out what she had done?

11. How have Marguerite's feelings for Percy changed and what does she think of his intelligence? (Do you think this is ironic foreshadowing and why or why not?)

12. What does she really think of her husband?

13. Describe Armand and Marguerite's relationship and tell about their life as brother and sister.

14. What is meant by "Secret Orchards?"

Chapter VIII
The Accredited Agent

1. What does how Marguerite feel about her brother say about the relationship between Marguerite and Percy?

2. What are the good qualities Marguerite says Percy has?

3. How long after their marriage was it that Marguerite tells Percy what she had done concerning the Marquis de St. Cry?

4. What was Armand's connection to the Marquis?

5. What was St. Cry trying to do which would be construed as treasonous to France in the state it finds itself?

Vocabulary:
utopian: _____
coterie: _____
malady: _____
snuff: _____
pernicious: _____

6. What has Marguerite done to St. Cry?

7. How did Percy react when Marguerite confessed to him her involvement?

8. How does Marguerite feel as she heads back to the Inn? What does she hear and see?

9. Who is this man that calls her by her French maiden name?

10. How does Marguerite feel when she sees him?

11. Where have we seen him previously?

12. Why does she stay outside and talk with the man?

13. What does Chauvelin prescribe to Marguerite that would help her "malady"- "ennui."

14. What does he want her to do?

15. What does Marguerite say about what is happening all around England because of the Scarlet Pimpernel?

16. Why does Chauvelin say the Scarlet Pimpernel is the most bitter enemy of men like Armand St. Juste?

Vocabulary:

ennui: _____

enigmatic: _____
_____

emigres: _____
_____

ostentatious: _____

humanity: _____

17. Who is Mr. Pitt?

18. What does Chauvelin say about the Scarlet Pimpernel especially about his intellect?

19. What does he want Marguerite to do?

20. What is her stance on the Revolution and how does she feel about the tactics of the french and what does she fear for her brother?

21. What are Marguerite's inner thoughts about the League of the Scarlet Pimpernel?

22. What does she think of their leader?

23. What is the possible ironic foreshadowing the author uses at this point in the story?

24. What stands between Marguerite and what Chauvelin purposes?

25. What will Chauvelin do when he finds the Scarlet Pimpernel?

26. What metaphor is used to describe Chauvelin as Marguerite pulls away from him?

27. What is Marguerite's response to him?

28. How does he lure her back?

29. Does his jab word to induce her to help him?

30. What is Chauvelin's reaction to her answer?

Chapter IX
The Outrage

1. Describe the setting later that night.

2. Describe the scene at the Fisherman's Rest including the characters.

3. Who does Sit Andrew dream about as he stares into the fire?

Vocabulary:

dexterous: _____

ingenuity: _____

peremptorily: _____

pinioned: _____

4. What does Sir Antony ask Andrew?

5. Who is going on the next "journey."

6. About what are they talking?

7. What is the story Andrew tells his friend?

8. What is the "mission" Tony will go on and with when?

9. What is the shocking revelation made about Armand St. Just?

10. Do the League and the Scarlet Pimpernel know about Chauvelin? Do they know who he is yet?

11. What or who is in the room with them and why don't they notice?

12. What happens next to Andrew and Antony?

13. Who is the mashed leader of the spies?

14. What has Chauvelin obtained in this little altercation as Marguerite and Percy ride away, enjoying the stars and silence in their carriage?

Chapter X
In the Opera Box

1. Who are the three important men of England present at the Opera and who is the "one extra?"

2. Who are the "foreign faces" present at the Opera and by what are they distracted?

3. How does the Comtesse de Tourney look and for whom might Suzanne be looking?

4. What news does Lord Granville bring of France?

5. What do the ladies suspect of Chauvelin?

Vocabulary:
arid: _____

apathetically: _____

6. What does Lady Portarles think of the Comtesse's dislike for Lady Blakeney?

7. What does "frou-frou" and is that a word we still use today?

8. Describe Marguerite at the Opera.

9. How does Marguerite react to Chauvelin's intrusion?

10. What happens that changes Marguerite's previous state of happiness to one of dread?

11. Does Marguerite know what her brother does?

12. What does Marguerite decipher that Chauvelin wants her to do?

13. What does the scrap of paper say?

14. What was arranged for Lord Antony and Andrew's escape and for what reasons were they "let go."

15. What does Chauvelin want Lady Blakeney to do and what will he give in exchange?

16. From whom does Marguerite think to get help?

17. Why does she change her mind?

Chapter XI
Lord Granville's Ball

1. Describe the guests at Lord Granville's Ball.

2. What are the Spetember Massacres and the Reign of Terror?

3. What is Chauvelin's opinion of England?

4. Describe Chauvelin's political position and opinion.

5. What does Chauvelin hope to do with the Scarlet Pinpernel, what does he ascribe to him, and what has he promised his colleagues in regards to him?

6. Who cause a moment of hushed conversation as they enter?

7. Who does Lord Granville present to the people at the Ball?

8. How does the Prince of Wales great and accept Chauvelin?

9. Who else does Lord Granville present to the Prince?

10. What does the Prince say about the Comtesse?

11. Explain the sarcasim in the Prince's introduction of the Comtesse to Lady Blakeney.

12. Describe how the Prince views the Scarlet Pimpernel.

13. How does Sir Percy break the tension growing in the room?

Chapter XII
The Scrap of Paper

1. Does Marguerite get help from Sir Percy? Why or why not?

2. What is the latest thing Sir Percy does that drives Marguerite crazy?

3. Where does Percy go and what is Marguerite left to do?

4. When Sir Andrew and Sir Antony come in, where does Sir Antony go first?

5. What does Marguerite wonder as she gazes around the room and what does she want?

6. How does Marguerite know the Scarlet Pimpernel is at the Ball?

7. Who does she watch?

8. Who does Marguerite see giving a slip of paper to Sir Andrew?

9. How does Marguerite get close to Sir Andrew and how does she obtain the note?

10. How does she obtain a chance to read it and does Sir Andrew know that she has and tell why he doesn't think she has after all?

Chapter XIII
Either- Or

1. Describe how Marguerite finds herself in the room with Andrew.

2. What does Marguerite see on the note that Andew is reading and what does she hope to do?

3. What did Sir Andrew think briefly of Marguerite and how has she managed to quelle any suspicions he may have had?

4. How does the Prince of Wales feel about Sir Percy and Lady Blakeney and what literary device could "this life would be a dreary desert without your smiles and his sallies," be?

Chapter XIV
One O'clock Precisely

1. How does dinner go?

2. For what does Marguerite hope?

3. What has Marguerite decided to do and what does she ask of Lord Fancourt and why?

4. What do Chauvelin and Lady Blakeney discuss?

5. What is Chauvelin's plan?

Vocabulary:
indefatigable: _____
_____

6. What is the significance of "Le chat gris" and what is the exact translation of the name?

7. What is the deal Chauvelin gives Marguerite concerning St. Just?

8. What does Chauvelin determine from the chairs in the dining room?

9. What does Chauvelin think he has set he has set for the Scarlet Pimpernel.

10. Who does Chauvelin find asleep on the sofa and what does he do?

Chapter XV
Doubt

1. What is Lady Blakeney thinking as she sits and waits in the drawing room?

2. When Lord Fancourt returns she hasn't been thinking of Sir Percy at all but has digressed and imagined herself where and when?

3. Where does Lord Fancourt say he has found Percy?

4. What are the implications of this and does Lady Blakeney even realize it? What does she think about the mission of Chauvelin to find the Scarlet Pimpernel has turned.

5. How is Chauvelin acting when Marguerite sees him on the stairs and describe their conversation that follows.

6. What is his promise to her?

7. What is Marguerite's only hope?

8. What is the metaphor of Lady Blakeney and the throng of people that always surround her?

9. What metaphor does Chauvelin use to describe his solving the mystery of the identity of the Scarlet Pimpernel?

10. Why had Sir Andrew not come to the meeting place? What was Sir Percy doing there? What does Chauvelin think? Does Sir Percy suspect anything?

XVI
Richmond

1. What mood does Orczy set for the drive home and what are some of the examples that aid it?

   Vocabulary:

   foibles: _____

   _____

2. What are Marguerite's thoughts on the way home?

   fanatic: _____

   _____

   _____

   aureole: _____

   _____

3. What is the mood of the scene at their house and what are the examples of it?

4. Describe the Blakeney's home/ house in great detail or draw a picture of it and label.

   Richmond

5. What do the both do upon arriving home?

6. How does Marguerite feel?

7. How do they both think the other one feels about themselves?

8. What does Marguerite ask Percy?

9. Did she love him when he loved her? Why does she marry him?

10. What happened to his love for her?

11. What does she now tell him about her involvement in the St. Cry affair that she has never told him because of her pride?

12. What does Marguerite realize after she pours her heart out to him and does his expression and countenance change?

13. Describe the misunderstanding that happened between them.

14. What is happening?

15. Why doesn't Percy comfort Marguerite?

16. Why don't they just kiss and make up?

17. What does he do once she has finally gone?

XVIII
Farewell

1. What does Marguerite now realize about her love for Percy?

2. After she dozes for an hour, what wakens her?

3. What does she find and what does it say?

4. What does she do and why?

5. Why is she suspicious and where does he finally admit he is going?

6. What does she learn about his foolishness?

7. And how is she now behaving foolishly?

XVIII
The Mysterious Device

1. Does Marguerite know anything at all about what Sir Percy is really doing? Is she at all worried about him or her brother and should she be?

2. What was Marguerite planning for the day and how has she managed to get the Comtesse to agree to letting Suzanne come?

3. What does Marguerite think is in Sir Percy's study?

4. Why are all the doors to Sir Percy's rooms standing open on this fine October morning... the study being one of them and what does Marguerite desire to do?

5. Orczy alludes to Bluebeard's wife. Find out what she discovers in this French fairy tale and what does she find behind the door at the end of the hall. (What does this say about the French if this story is considered a Fairy Tale?)

6. What does Marguerite learn of Sir Percy just by being in his study?

7. Describe in great detail or draw and label Sir Percy's study. How does it contradict everyone's perception of him?

Lord Blakeney's Study

8. What feeling is creeping in on Marguerite and what does she find as she is leaving the study?

XIX
The Scarlet Pimpernel

1. Where does Marguerite go to think about the thing she has found in Sir Percy's study?

2. Who finds her there?

3. Who else does Suzanne remind Marguerite needs to be saved by the Scarlet Pimpernel?

4. Finally Marguerite figures it out- how? Who is really the clever one who is the fool?

5. Why does she think Percy never told her?

Vocabulary:
poignancy: _____
_____
efface: _____
_____

6. Now we see the irony of the situation. What is it?

7. What was in the letter for Marguerite?

8. What does Marguerite plan to do?

XX
The Friend

1. All the sudden, Marguerite has a new opinion and feeling toward her husband. What is it? How is it different than before?

2. Whose help does she seek, how does he react, what does he ask, and what is her response?

3. How many helpers are in the League of the Scarlet Pimpernel?

4. What is Marguerite's plan?

XXI
Suspense

1. How does Jellyband react when Lady Blakeney shows up at the Fisherman's Rest?

2. What ideas does Jellyband have regarding Lady Blakeney and Sir Andrew?

3. Does Marguerite finally think about what others may think of her midnight rendezvous and what does she herself think about her appearances?

4. What does Sir Andrew say about their being able to cross to France that night?

5. How does Sir Andrew try to put Jellyband's fears to rest?

Vocabulary:

alacrity: _____

quandary: _____

sedulously: _____

6. Why doesn't Sir Andrew just "take Chauvelin out" and what is the difference in the laws of England and France on this matter?

7. What does Sir Andrew do to pass the time with Lady Blakeney?

8. What does Orczy say about the sea as Lady Blakeney meditates on it as she tries to go to sleep?

XXII
Calais

1. Can Marguerite and Sir Andrew leave in the morning and why or why not?

2. When are they finally able to leave?

    Vocabulary:
    impedimenta: _____
    _____
    dilapidated: _____

3. What is the irony in the fact that it is Sir Andrew who is the one by Lady Blakeney's side when she is in great trouble?

    incontinently: _____
    _____

4. Who do we know how Orczy feels about the Revolution in France?

5. What color caps do the Frenchmen wear, what is a tricolor cockade, and what kinds of looks do the people of Calais wear upon their Faces?

53

6. Who are always welcome guests at the French taverns of Calais and Bologna? Why?

7. What is the metaphor Orcy uses to describe how Lady Blakeney feels as she is immediately on her way to meet her husband?

8. Describe in detail or draw the setting of the Chat Gris.

The Chat Gris

9. How do the Frenchies and especially the tavern keeper feel about the Anglais (the English?)

10. Describe the woman sitting in the corner stirring the soup.

11. For what does Sir Antony ask?

12. How does the tavern keeper feel about serving the aristocrats?

13. How does Marguerite feel about eating food from the tavern?

14. Describe Monsier Brogard's attitude toward Marguerite and Sir Andrew.

15. Why does Lady Blakeney tell Sir Andrew to be nice to the tavern helper?
16. How does Sir Andrew flatter Brogard?

17. How does Brogard make fun of Sir Percy?

18. How is Lady Blakeney reacting to the whole pantomime and how do they think Percy is going around town? How does this make Marguerite feel?

19. Where does Brogard say Percy went?

20. How does Sir Andrew keep Lady Blakeney from giving herself away? How is Brogard transformed in Lady Blakeney's eyes at that point?

21. How does Brogard act toward Lady Blakeney in general as a new, equal citizen?

XXIII
Hope

1. Of what is Sir Andrew cautious or fearful?

2. Does Marguerite seem to care?

3. Where has Sir Andrew seen Chauvelin?

4. What does Marguerite realize?

5. What is the Scarlet Pimpernel's plan?

6. How long do Lady Blakeney and Sir Andrew have to find Percy?

7. What is Lady Blakeney's plan and what does Sir Andrew say will thwart her plan?

8. What has Marguerite forgotten?

9. What is her resolution and what are she and Sir Andrew to do?

10. Where does Marguerite go to wait for Sir Percy or Sir Andrew to return?

XXIV
The Death Trap

1. How does Brogard get ready for the next guest and who does Lady Blakeney assume it is? How does Brogard seem to feel about the next guest and how do you know?

2. Describe the scene of Brogard preparing for the guest, Marguerite hiding in the loft, etc.

3. What does Marguerite think of while she sits in the straw and waits?

4. All this anticipation is leading up to some climatic point- what could it be?

Vocabulary:
factotum: _____
_____
_____

5. Who comes in to the tavern that Marguerite thinks will be her husband?

6. As Chauvelin waits for Desgas to report back that they've found Percy, who comes into the tavern?

Chapter XXV
The Eagle and the Fox

1. Describe the scene between Percy and Chauvelin.

2. Why doesn't Chauvelin strike?

3. What are the thoughts racing through Marguerite's head?

4. How does Percy exit, seemingly, just in the nick of time?

Chapter XXVI
The Jew

1. Describe the cart driver in great detail or draw and label. What use is he to Chauvelin?

The Cart Driver

2. Where does the cart driver take Chauvelin?

3. What story does he tell Chauvelin about the carts and the Englishman?

4. How does Chauvelin feel about him?

5. Describe the road they are taking and where they go.

Chapter XXVII
On the Track

1. Describe what Marguerite does after everyone leaves the tavern. Where does she go and how does she get there?

2. Describe what is happening inside the hut and surrounding the hut.

3. Why don't the soldiers arrest the four refugees inside the hut and who are they?

4. What does the foot soldier report to Chauvelin about the hut and what is their plan?

Chapter XXVIII
The Pere Blanchards Hut

1. Describe how Marguerite gets close enough to overhear Chauvelin.

2. What is the metaphor Chauvelin use to explain how he wants his men to be while surrounding the hut and what are their very specific instructions?

3. What do they do with the cart driver?

4. Finally Chauvelin asks the man's name. What is it?

5. What is Chauvelin originally order to Benjamin and how does Benjamin manage to get himself closer to the hut and how does he go there?

6. What does Marguerite see in the sea?

7. What does Marguerite try to do and how is she stopped.

Chapter XXIX
Trapped

1. Where are Benjamin and Marguerite now?

2. What are the thoughts going through Marguerite's head and how does Chauvelin torment her?

3. Does Marguerite scream out to warn Percy or the others in the hut?

4. What do they all hear in the silence of the night that seems very ludicrous?

Chapter XXX
The Schooner

Find a picture of a schooner from the late 1700's and draw or paste it here.

1. What courage does Marguerite now show and describe the scene that unfolds.

2. How do the soldiers find the hut upon entering it?

3. What has happened to the fugitives and why were they not stopped and caught?

4. How have the escaped?

5. What does Chauvelin find inside the hut and what does it explain?

6. Why do yo think Chauvelin has been able to acquire the note?

7. Where does the note say the fugitives have gone and where does it say the Scarlet Pimpernel will meet them?

Vocabulary:

factotum: _____
_____

anathema: _____
_____

8. What does Chauvelin immediately do?

9. How does he have Benjamin treated before he leaves and why?

10. In what condition is Marguerite?

11. Why does Chauvelin think he can leave the two of them there until morning?

12. Why does Chauvelin punish Benjamin so badly?

13. What rouses Lady Blakeney from her unconscious state?

14. How does Chauvelin depart from her?

XXXI
The Escape

1. What thoughts race through Marguerite's mind as she lays on the rocks- defeated?

2. What rouses her?

3. How long does it seem to take before she realizes who the "Englishman" is and whence come the sounds of his voice?

4. How is Percy comical yet heroic even in this scene after having been beaten to a pulp by Chauvelin's men?

5. How does Marguerite get his ropes off his wrists?

6. Who finally returns and what means?

7. What has he been doing?

8. What are their next plans and how are they carried out?

9. On board the schooner, what is Percy able to do?

10. Lastly- how do the Blakeney's look at the wedding of Sir Andrew and Mlle. Suzanne?

11. Does Chauvelin ever come to England again? Why or why not?

Essay Questions

Answer the following questions in paragraph form. Give proofs to support your answers and examples to support your proofs.

1. If you were Chauvelin, what would you have done differently to capture the Scarlet Pimpernel?

2. Does Percy know everything Marguerite has done since the ball and how does this make him feel? Does he blame her or himself?

3. Would you have joined the League of the Scarlet Pimpernel? Why or why not?

4. What do you think about the French Revolution and why?

5. Why do you think a Revolution ever occurred in England?

6. What is the result today? Give many details.

7. Is the French Revolution comparable to the American Revolution? Why or why not?

8. How do yo think the lower classed in France felt compared to those in england and why would they feel differently?

9. Is a class system a good or bad thing? Give reasons to support your answers.

10. Is there a class system in America today and how is it the same or different than those in England or France during the mid 1700's?

Creative Writing Assignments

Write a short story about a Scarlet Pimpernel rescue. The rescue has to be from Paris, walled and gated Paris, to England. You are rescuing a family from the guillotine. Describe the imagery and characterization in great detail.

Draw your Scarlet Pimpernel in costume here, escaping France...

Essay Topics

Choose one topic from each section on which to write a five paragraph essay. (See appendix for essay outlines and instructions for writing a good essay.)

Literary Topics

- *Who are the main protagonist and antagonist of the novel? Who carries the emotional weight of the novel and who is against he/she and how?*
- *How does d'Orcy develop imagery to aid setting mood in the novel?*
- *Why doesn't Chauvelin have to die at the end of the novel for a successful resolution?*
- *How is nobility vs. the masses a theme for the novel and on which side is d'Orczy?*
- *How is guilt vs. redemtion a recurring theme in the novel?*
- *How does d'Orcy develop characterization through dual identities throughout the novel?*
- *Discuss the symbolism of the scarlet pimpernel- and the choice in that particular flower to represent the hero and how does it (or not) fit Percy*
- *How is Chauvelin a threating villian even though he never engages in combat and likewise, how is Percy a credible adversary even though he never engages in physical battle?*

Essay Outline- Write your sentences in the outline-

Quote from book or other... (indented on both sides and italicized)

I. Introductory Paragraph

    A) Grabber-

    B) Grabber-

    C) Introduce the book and Author

    D) Main Idea

    E) Thesis Statement (Including three prongs, or reasons, which support your Main Idea.)

II. First Paragraph of the Body

    A) Grabber- Link 1st prong of Thesis statement to paragraph

    B) Proof

    C) proof

    D) proof

    E) Conclusion or segway to next paragraph

III. Second Paragraph of the Body

    A) Grabber- Link 2nd prong of Thesis statement to paragraph

    B) Proof

    C) proof

    D) proof

    E) Conclusion or segway to next paragraph

IV. Third Paragraph of the Body

    A)   Grabber- Link 3rd prong of Thesis statement to paragraph

    B)   Proof

    C)   proof

    D)   proof

    E)   Conclusion or segway to next paragraph

V. Concluding Paragraph

    A)   Intro to paragraph restating thesis statement

    B)   summary of proof

    C)   summary of proof

    D)   summary of proof

    E)   concluding statement

Check your sentences to make sure you don't just have subject/ verb simple sentences.

How many compound sentences do you have? _____

How many complex sentences do you have? _____

How many compound/ complex sentences do you have? _____

How many sentences start with an adjective?_____

How many sentences start with an adverb?_____

How many sentences start with a prepositional phrase?_____

How many adverb clauses do you have and which types? _____

How many adjective clauses do you have and which types? _____

How many being or linking verbs do you use..... _____ Change them to action verbs!

How many good descriptive words do you use... adverbs? _____ adjectives? _____

How many direct quotes do you have from the book do you have to prove your points? ____

How many examples do you have from the book to prove your point?_____

Do you have a good quote to start your paper that is relevant to your Main Idea?_____

Does your Introductory paragraph grab the readers attention? _____

Is the name of the book italicized if typed or underlined if handwritten?_____

Are your 3 prongs and obvious?_____

Are the prongs in the same order as the order of supporting paragraphs and clear? ____

Do you do a good job proving your prongs,or reasons for your Main Idea? _____

Does your concluding paragraph restate your Main Idea and Proofs in a Way that is not redundant and boring?_____

Write rough draft on following pages and type final copy.

Historical Topics

Choose one topic to write a five paragraph essay

- Write a persuasive essay conveying your opinion on the French Revolution
- How is the French Revolution alike or different from the American Revolution?
- Write an essay comparing and contrasting the classes in 1700 France
- Write an essay comparing and contrasting the classes in 1700 England

Essay Outline

Quote from book or other... *(indented on both sides and italicized)*

I. Introductory Paragraph

-
-
-
  - Main Idea-
  - Thesis Statement-

II. First Paragraph of the Body

- Grabber- 1st prong
- Proof-
- proof-
- proof-
- Conclusion or segway to next paragraph-

III. Second Paragraph of the Body

1. Grabber- Link 2nd prong
2. Proof-
3. proof-
4. proof-
5. Conclusion or segway to next paragraph

IV. Third Paragraph of the Body

    1)   Grabber- Link 3rd prong

    2)   Proof-

    3)   proof-

    4)   proof

    5)   Conclusion or segway to next paragraph

V. Concluding Paragraph

    1. Intro to paragraph restating thesis statement

    2. summary of proof

    3. summary of proof

    4. summary of proof

    5. concluding statement

Check your sentences to make sure you don't just have subject/ verb simple sentences.

How many compound sentences do you have? _____

How many complex sentences do you have? _____

How many compound/ complex sentences do you have? _____

How many sentences start with an adjective?_____

How many sentences start with an adverb?_____

How many sentences start with a prepositional phrase?_____

How many adverb clauses do you have and which types? _____

How many adjective clauses do you have and which types? _____

How many being or linking verbs do you use..... _____ Change them to action verbs!

How many good descriptive words do you use... adverbs? _____ adjectives? _____

How many direct quotes do you have from the book do you have to prove your points? ____

How many examples do you have from the book to prove your point?_____

Do you have a good quote to start your paper that is relevant to your Main Idea?_____

Does your Introductory paragraph grab the readers attention? _____

Is the name of the book italicized if typed or underlined if handwritten?_____

Are your 3 prongs and obvious?_____

Are the prongs in the same order as the order of supporting paragraphs and clear? ____

Do you do a good job proving your prongs,or reasons for your Main Idea? _____

Does your concluding paragraph restate your Main Idea and Proofs in a Way that is not redundant and boring?_____

Write rough draft on following pages and type final copy.

Choose on topic on which to write a Research Paper. Make a presentation board to go along with your paper and be prepared to share your work. (Use MLA writing style.)

- Madame d'Orczy
- The French Revolution
- King George
- London of the late 1700's (including, Inns, Balls, the Opera, class system, etc.)
- France of the late 1700's (including Inns, Balls, Operas, Prisons, the class system, etc.)
- King Louis XVI and Marie Antoinette
- Versaille
- The Reign of Terror and the Guillotine

- Paper must be typed- not handwritten.
-
- List at least five references three of which are not on the internet.

Some sources are prohibited because of their basic nature or lack of credibility. General encyclopedias and Wikipedia should not be used as final sources of information and should be starting points only; no research paper should cite information from them.

- Use notecards for taking notes.
- Cite works on a works cited page at the end of paper
- Use footnotes.
- Length must be at least 1200 words and not more than 1600

(Not including works cited page)

Your grade on the research paper will be distributed as follows:

Topic	5
Note Cards	10
Outline	5
Rough Draft	15
Final Copy	**65**
Total	100

In addition, the grade on your final paper will be distributed as follows:

Content	25
MLA Style	15
Mechanics	15
Works Cited	10

Points are earned on the date that each section is due. For example, if you do not have your note cards finished on _____, you will not earn those 10 points.

DUE DATES

Topic	_____
Note Cards	_____
Outline	_____
Rough Draft	_____
Final Copy	_____

Vocabulary Assignment

Here is a complete list of all the vocabulary words from the book.

Satiety	Inane	Reiterate
citoyen	inanities	dexterous
pluck	imperturbable	ingenuity
audacity	bonhomie	peremptorily
impudent	coterie	pinioned
elusive	bantam	arid
peremptory	choleric	apathetically
sarcastic	utopian	indefatigable
anent	coterie	foibles
rueful	malady	fanatic
rubland	snuff	aureole
dessinated	pernicious	poignancy
preposterous	ennui	efface
plebeian	enigmatic	alacrity
sang-froid	emigres	quandary
soupçon	ostentatious	sedulously
scion	humanity	impedimenta
insolence	insinuatingly	dilapidated
fichu	contempt	incontinently
	equanimity	anathema

*Please note- some of these words are French.... they may not be in an English dictionary. However, there are some French words and phrases that have been adopted into the English language and you may find them as English words; deja vu, buffet, promenade, etc.

Use the graph below to make a crossword puzzle of the vocabulary words from the novel. Use the definitions as questions or clues for the words. (Use as many words as you can! Be ready to share your crossword puzzle with a friend.)

	Across		Down
1		1	
2		2	
3		3	
4		4	
5		5	
6		6	
7		7	
8		8	
9		9	
10		10	
11		11	
12		12	
13		13	
14		14	
15		15	
16		16	
17		17	
18		18	
19		19	
20		20	
21		21	
22		22	
23		23	
24		24	
25		25	
26		26	
27		27	
28		28	
29		29	

Grammar Challenge

Find examples from the novel of each of the following grammar topics.

Independent Clause

Dependent Clause

Simple Sentence

Compound Sentence

Complex Sentence

Compound Complex Sentence

Adverb Clause

Adjective Clause

Prepositional Phrase

Gerund/ Gerund Phrase

Infinitive

Split Infinitive

Helping Verb

Linking or Being Verb

Action Verb

Adverb

Preposition

Adjective
    Article
      Gerund

Conjunction

Literary Challenge

Find an example of each from the novel.

See the appendix for definitions of each.

allegory	
alliteration	
allusion	
assonance	
characterization	
consonance	
flashback	
foreshadowing	
hyperbole	
imagery	
ironic foreshadowing	
irony	
metaphor	
motif	
onomatopoeia	
personification	
plot	
simile	
symbolism	
theme	

Fill in what each of the following parts of the story are.

See the appendix for definitions of each.

Exposition	
Rising action	
Climax	
Falling action	
Resolution/ denouement	
Main characters	
Supporting characters	
antagonist	
conflict	
dialogue	
diction	
genre	
plot	
Point of view	
protagonist	
setting	
theme	
tone	

Appendix

Literary Terms and Definitions

allegory	A symbolic fictional narrative that conveys a secondary meaning not explicitly set forth in the literal narrative
alliteration	Repetition of the initial consonant sounds of words: "Peter Piper picked a peck of pickled peppers."
allusion	A reference to something well-known that exists outside the literary work
assonance	Repetition of vowel sounds followed by different consonant sounds
characterization	The manner in which the author develops characters and their personalities
consonance	The repetition of consonant sounds specifically in the middle or end of words
flashback	The method of returning to an earlier point in time for the purpose of of making the present clear.
foreshadowing	Hint of what is to come in a literary work.
hyperbole	Extreme exaggeration to add meaning
imagery	Language that appeals to the five senses
ironic foreshadowing	The opposite of the hint that is given of what is to come
irony	Dramatic- when the reader or audience knows something a character does not Situational- when there is a disparity between what is expected and what actually occurs Verbal- when the speaker says one thing but means the opposite
metaphor	A figure of speech in which a word or phrase denoting one kind of object or action is used in place of another to suggest likeness or analogy between them
motif	A recurring feature of a literary work that is related to a theme
onomatopoeia	Use of a word whose sound imitates its meaning: "BOOM" "hiss"

oxymoron	Phrase that consists of two words that are contradictory
personification	A figure of speech in which non-human things are given human characteristics
simile	A direct comparison of dissimilar objects, usually using like or as: "I wandered lonely as a cloud."
suspense	Technique that keeps the reader guessing what will happen next
symbolism	One thing- object, person, place- used to represent something else

Parts of a Story

Exposition	The essential background information at the beginning of a literary work
Rising action	The development of conflict and complications in a literary work
Climax	The turning point in a literary work
Falling action	The results or effects of the climax of a literary work
Resolution/ denouement	End of a literary work in which the loose ends are tied up and any questions are answered
Main characters	The character or characters in a literary work which take up most of the story
Supporting characters	Any other characters in the work which aid the main character
antagonist	The character that is the source of conflict in the story- usually the villan
conflict	Struggle between two or more opposing forces/ person to person, nature, society, self, fate/God
dialogue	Direct speech between characters in a literary work
diction	Word choice to create a specific effect
genre	Type or category in which a literary work belongs
plot	The sequence of events in a literary work
Point of view	The vantage point or perspective from which the work is told 1st person- Told from the main characters point of view/ Uses I 3rd person- Told from the narrator point of view fromoutside of the story/ uses he, she, they
protagonist	The main character of the story, often the hero
setting	Where the story takes place and the time period of the story
theme	The underlying main idea of a literary work which states the opinion or makes a statement about the subject
tone	The author's attitude toward the subject of a work

Essay Outline and Instructions

Quote from book or other... (Indented on both sides and single spaced and italicized)

I. Introductory Paragraph

    A) Grabber-

    B) Grabber-

    C) Introduce the book and Author

    D) Main Idea

    E) Thesis Statement (Including three prongs, or reasons, which support your Main Idea.)

II. First Paragraph of the Body

    A) Grabber- Link 1st prong of Thesis statement to paragraph- Topic Sentence

    B) Proof

    C) proof

    D) proof

    E) Conclusion or seaway to next paragraph

III. Second Paragraph of the Body

    A) Grabber- Link 2nd prong of Thesis statement to paragraph- Topic Sentence

    B) Proof

    C) proof

    D) proof

    E) Conclusion or segway to next paragraph

IV. Third Paragraph of the Body

    A)   Grabber- Link 3rd prong of Thesis statement to paragraph- Topic Sentence

    B)   Proof

    C)   proof

    D)   proof

    E)   Conclusion or segway to next paragraph

V. Concluding Paragraph

    A)   Intro to paragraph restating thesis statement- Topic Sentence

    B)   summary of proof

    C)   summary of proof

    D)   summary of proof

    E)   concluding statement

Grading Checklist for Essays

- Is your essay five paragraphs long with five to seven sentences in each paragraph?
- In your typed copy are the lines double spaced and make sure there are NO spaces skipped in between paragraphs.
- Is your essay written in present tense?
- Is your essay written in third person?

- *Check your sentences to make sure you don't just have subject/ verb simple sentences.*
- *How many compound sentences do you have? _____*
- *How many complex sentences do you have? _____*
- *How many compound/ complex sentences do you have? _____*
- *How many sentences start with an adjective?_____*
- *How many sentences start with an adverb?_____*
- *How many sentences start with a prepositional phrase?_____*
- *How many adverb clauses do you have and which types? _____*
- *How many adjective clauses do you have and which types? _____*
- *How many being or linking verbs do you use..... _____ Change them to action verbs!*
- *How many good descriptive words do you use... adverbs? _____ adjectives? _____*
- *How many direct quotes do you have from the book do you have to prove your points? ___*
- *How many examples do you have from the book to prove your point?_____*
- *Do you have a good quote to start your paper that is relevant to your Main Idea?_____*
- *Does your Introductory paragraph grab the readers attention? _____*
- *Is the name of the book italicized if typed or underlined if handwritten?_____*

- *Are your 3 prongs and obvious?_____*
- *Are the prongs in the same order as the order of supporting paragraphs and clear? ____*
- *Do you do a good job proving your prongs, or reasons for your Main Idea? _____*
- *Does your concluding paragraph restate your Main Idea and Proofs in a Way that is not redundant and boring?_____*
- *Grammar- Are all of your sentences complete sentences, your punctuation correct, and your words spelled correctly and capitalization in correct?*

If you have managed to answer yes to each of the preceding points and have examples of each requirement give yourself an A!

If you cannot answer yes and give an example of each point, go back and fix your essay. Edit your essay and reprint a final copy and regrade it making sure you can answer yes to each point.

Grammar Rules

Subject- The part of the sentence which provides who or what is doing the action- a noun part of the sentence

Predicate- The part of the sentence which provides what the subject is or is doing- a verb part of the sentence

Independent Clause- a group of words that can stand on its own and make sense, having a subject and a predicate

Dependent Clause- a group of words that cannot stand on its own and make sense

Simple Sentence- a sentence with one subject part and one predicate part

Compound Subject- a sentence consisting of two subjects joined by a conjunction

Compound Predicate- a sentence consisting of two predicate parts joined by a conjunction

Compound sentence- two sentences joined by a conjunction or semi-colon

Complex Sentence- a sentence having both an independent clause and a dependent clause.

Compound Complex Sentence- a compound sentence and a complex sentence in one

Adverb Clause- a group of words that modify a verb

Adjective Clause- a group of words that modifies a noun (including phrases that begin with who and which)

Prepositional Phrase- a group of words that tells where and can either modify a noun or an adverb and begins with one of the following words- (a preposition) and ends with a noun. A prepositional phrase can be used as either an adjective or an adverb. When used as an adjective it will tell which one; when used as an adverb it will tell where, how, or when.

Memorize the following prepostions;

about	*below*	*excepting*	*off*	*toward*
above	*beneath*	*for*	*on*	*under*
across	*beside(s)*	*from*	*onto*	*underneath*
after	*between*	*in*	*out*	*until*
against	*beyond*	*in front of*	*outside*	*up*
along	*but*	*inside*	*over*	*upon*
among	*by*	*in spite of*	*past*	*up to*
around	*concerning*	*instead of*	*regarding*	*with*
at	*despite*	*into*	*since*	*within*
because of	*down*	*like*	*through*	*without*
before	*during*	*near*	*throughout*	*with regard to*
behind	*except*	*of*	*to*	*with respect to*

Gerund/ Gerund Phrase- a group of words beginning with an ing verb which is used to describe something- as an adjective i.e. *Running to the car, she dropped her keys.*

Infinitive/ Infinitive Phrase- an infinitive is a group of words consisting of the word to and a simple verb. An infinitive phrase is a group of words beginning with the infinitive which is used as a noun.

Split Infinitive- to put an adverb on adjective in between the to and the verb in an infinite. The most well-known split infinitive ever.... "'to boldly go!' where no man has gone before.........."

Helping Verb- a verb which helps an another verb

Linking or Being Verb- a helping verb which links the subject part of the sentence to the predicate part of the sentence or tells what state a subject is in

Action Verb- a verb which shows action

Adverb- a word or phrase that modifies a verb

Preposition- see above- certain words that tell when, where, how, or which one. Just have to memorize them.

Adjective- a word or phrase that describes a noun
    Article- the, an, a
    Gerund- an ing verb that modifies a noun

Conjunctions- and, or, but; joins words, phrases, or clauses

Made in the USA
Coppell, TX
29 January 2023